CW00495575

GALE
CENGAGE Learning

Poetry for Students, Volume 37

Project Editor: Sara Constantakis Rights Acquisition and Management: Jacqueline Flowers, Sari Gordon, Kelly Quin, Robyn Young Composition: Evi Abou-El-Seoud Manufacturing: Rhonda Dover

Imaging: John Watkins

Product Design: Pamela A. E. Galbreath, Jennifer Wahi Content Conversion: Katrina Coach Product Manager: Meggin Condino

For product information and technology assistance, contact us at **Gale Customer Support, 1-800-877-4253**.
For permission to use material from this text or product, submit all requests online at www.cengage.com/permissions.
Further permissions questions can be emailed to **permissionrequest@cengage.com** While every effort has been made to ensure the reliability of the information presented in this publication, Gale, a part of Cengage Learning, does not guarantee the accuracy of the data contained herein. Gale accepts no payment for listing; and inclusion in the publication of any organization, agency, institution, publication, service, or individual does not imply endorsement of the editors or publisher. Errors brought to the attention of the publisher and verified to the satisfaction of the publisher will be corrected in future editions.

Gale
27500 Drake Rd.
Farmington Hills, MI, 48331-3535

ISBN-13: 978-1-4144-6704-7
ISBN-10: 1-4144-6704-4
ISSN 1094-7019

This title is also available as an e-book.
ISBN-13: 978-1-4144-7388-8

ISBN-10: 1-4144-7388-5
Contact your Gale, a part of Cengage Learning sales representative for ordering information.

Printed in the United States of America
1 2 3 4 5 6 7 15 14 13 12 11

The New Colossus

Emma Lazarus

1883

Introduction

To commemorate the centennial of the Declaration of Independence, the people of France raised money to build the Statue of Liberty. The statue was to be a sign of friendship between France and the United States and a symbol of freedom and democracy. On this side of the Atlantic Ocean, the people of the United States raised money to build the pedestal upon which the huge statue would sit in the harbor of New York City. To help encourage people to donate to the cause, an auction was held. One of the items in that auction was Emma Lazarus's poem "The New Colossus."

The construction, shipment, and erection of the statue took longer than expected, so the centennial of the Declaration of Independence came and went before the statue was completely installed in 1886. And though Lazarus's poem was officially published at the auction in 1883, it did not become a part of the statue until 1903, after the poet's death. Without ceremony, a bronze tablet on which "The New Colossus" was engraved was finally attached to the interior wall of the pedestal.

Though the poem received little initial attention, today the words of Lazarus's poem (especially the last five lines) have become synonymous with the Statue of Liberty. It is through the power of Lazarus's "The New Colossus" that the statue stands not only for freedom and democracy but also as a welcoming beacon to immigrants who come to this country.

Author Biography

Lazarus is considered one of the first successful female Jewish poets in the United States. As David Lehman wrote in *Smithsonian* magazine, Lazarus was "a fascinating figure and a much more substantial poet than she has been given credit for." Though today she is primarily remembered for "The New Colossus," in the late nineteenth century she was considered an important American poet.

Lazarus was born in New York City on July 22, 1849, the fourth of seven children of Moshe and Esther Lazarus. Her parents were Sephardic Jews whose ancestors were exiled from Portugal and emigrated to New York during America's colonial period. As a child, she lived both in New York City and in Newport, Rhode Island. Lazarus was educated by private tutors. Her father, one of her biggest fans, was impressed by his daughter's early writings and supported her development as a poet. When Lazarus was seventeen, her father financed the private printing of a collection of her poems, called *Poems and Translations: Written between the Ages of Fourteen and Sixteen* (1866). Shortly after this publication appeared, Lazarus met Ralph Waldo Emerson, the famed American poet, who would, for a time, become her mentor. Though they would eventually part ways, Emerson is credited with helping Lazarus improve and develop her writing.

When Lazarus was twenty-two, her second

book, *Admetus and Other Poems* (1871) was published. Three years later, she published a novel, fictionalizing a story of the German author Johann Wolfgang von Goethe. The novel, *Alide: An Episode of Goethe's Life* (1874), was the only novel that Lazarus would write.

For the rest of her life, Lazarus focused on poetry and essays. Her poetry was often published in magazines, and the respect she earned with her writing was the reason she was sought by the committee responsible for raising funds for the pedestal upon which the Statue of Liberty would eventually stand. "The New Colossus" was engraved on a bronze plaque in 1903 and placed inside the walls of the pedestal.

Though she did not practice Judaism as an adult, Lazarus focused on the plight of Jews throughout the world during the latter part of her life, especially the challenges that Jewish immigrants faced and the anti-Semitism and persecution they faced in the late nineteenth century in Russia and Germany. It was her empathy for these European Jews that led her to become involved with immigrants, often visiting Ellis Island and talking to the new arrivals about their experiences. Her association with these immigrants influenced the overall theme of "The New Colossus."

In an effort to regain her physical and emotional strength following the death of her beloved father in the spring of 1885, Lazarus spent more than two years abroad, traveling to England,

France, and Italy. Unfortunately, the years overseas did not improve her health. She returned home exhausted and died in New York on November 19, 1887.

Poem Summary

Lines 1–8

"The New Colossus," a tribute to the Statue of Liberty, begins with an attention-getting statement that, together with the title, alludes to another large statue, the ancient Colossus of Rhodes. At one time, this Greek structure stood at the entrance to the harbor of the island of Rhodes, as the soon to be constructed Statue of Liberty would stand at the entrance to New York Harbor. Because of the similar roles that these two colossal statues would play as well as their related dimensions, the connection between the Colossus of Rhodes and the Statue of Liberty is easily made. In addition, the French sculptor Fre′ de′ ric-Auguste Bartholdi, who was commissioned to create the statue, had also connected the two statues in his mind. His ideas were inspired by the Colossus of Rhodes—by its large size, its position of prominence in the Rhodian harbor, and its powerful symbolism.

Though Lazarus was aware of the connection between the ancient Colossus of Rhodes and the Statue of Liberty, her ideas about the relationship between the two statues differed from Bartholdi's. Lazarus does not deny that the two colossal statues have elements in common; however, she suggests that there is a contrast between their surface form and their deeper meaning. She claims that the ties between the two statues exist only if one takes a hurried look at both. The statues may both be huge structures that grace harbors, but the similarities stop there. So with the first line of her poem, Lazarus makes it clear that, in her mind, Bartholdi's statue is actually nothing like the ancient Colossus. The poem will develop this theme throughout the octave, or the first eight lines, of this Italian sonnet. She will reflect on the Colossus of Rhodes, but the poem's main focus will be on the Statue of Liberty—the new colossus.

Media Adaptations

- American composer Irving Berlin wrote a song based on Lazarus's poem. Various versions of Berlin's composition "Give Me Your Tired and Your Poor" are performed on YouTube.com.
- Another version of Berlin's

composition based on" The New Colossus" was recorded on the album *Miss Liberty* (1991) and an MP3 music download of "Give Me Your Tired and Your Poor" can be found at Amazon.com.

"The New Colossus," describes the ancient colossus as being audacious, or boldly shameless. The ancient colossus, after all, was a statue of the Greek god Helios. This image implies that the statue has supernatural powers that were meant to frighten Rhodian enemies away from their harbor. Whereas the Colossus of Rhodes was more like a boastful bully, marking the statue with a sort of arrogance that a champion of war might display, the Statue of Liberty is something else. Although the poem has not yet specifically described the Statue of Liberty, readers have a hint of what the speaker of this poem in about to say. For example, because the speaker has already stated that the American statue is nothing like the Colossus of Rhodes, readers can infer that the speaker believes that the Statue of Liberty is neither bold nor arrogant.

In the second line, before the speaker of this poem identifies the attributes of the State of Liberty, she further describes the Rhodian statue. Because the Colossus of Rhodes was destroyed by an earthquake in 224 BCE, there is no authentic historical representation of the actual Greek statue. There are only widely varying written descriptions.

Lazarus adopted a popular description of the Colossus of Rhodes that some modern-day architects believe would have been impossible to construct. This depiction, some believe, had the male statue bridging the sides of the harbor at Rhodes with his torso, with one of his feet on one side of the water and the other on the opposite shore. This is a more aggressive pose, one that epitomizes the power of a mighty god who has won a great battle. Though the actual pose of the Colossus of Rhodes might have not been so emboldened, Lazarus is correct in stating that the great Colossus did symbolize victory in war.

It is in line 4 of the octave that the speaker finally introduces the statue that will soon stand on the American shores and begins to add details as to how the two statues differ from one another. As opposed to the male statue in Rhodes, the American statue is a female figure. The speaker implies that in the Statue of Liberty's hands, there are no weapons of war. Rather, there is a torch, a symbol of the power of fire or light. This power is different from the powerful weapons of war because it is not destructive. The torch represents a guiding light. The sculptor Bartholdi had named the statue "Liberty Enlightening the World." This title was chosen to praise the people of the United States for their accomplishment in creating and putting into place a working democratic government. The torch, for Bartholdi, was said to stand for enlightenment (in the sense of illumination or clarification), or a light being sent out to demonstrate the knowledge of how democracy should and could work. But

Lazarus interprets the Statue of Liberty and the statue's torch slightly differently. For her, the statue is the embodiment of a nurturer, a motherly figure. The torch, which represents her power, has been tamed. Unlike the ancient colossus who boasts of his war-like power, the Statue of Liberty constrains her strength and turns it into a beacon of light that not only guides shiploads of people to the shores of the United States but also welcomes them, changing the darkness of their journey into light.

In line 6 of the octave, Lazarus turns her attention to the immigrants who are coming to the American shores. She refers to them as exiles. And it is here in the sixth line that Lazarus more fully changes the symbolic image of the statue from one of celebrating democracy and freedom to one of nurturing lost souls. The statue becomes a mother figure who welcomes all the weary strangers coming to a new land. And she does so not with threats or warnings, but with outstretched arms. Her beacon is not only a guiding light that marks a safe passage; it is also a signal of full acceptance. Unlike the ancient Colossus whose fierce gaze looked upon the harbor with warnings to intruders, the Statue of Liberty has soft eyes that are watching over the new arrivals like a protective mother.

Lines 9–14

Line 9 marks the beginning of the sestet (the last six lines of an Italian sonnet) of Lazarus's poem. It is in the sestet that the speaker explains what the

Statue of Liberty represents by having the statue speak for herself, albeit with stone lips. She shouts to the ancient colossus to keep his famed magnificence to himself. The Statue of Liberty, obviously, wants nothing to do with the spectacle of battled victories. She is not about glorified display. In other words, she is not, the speaker emphasizes again, like the Colossus of Rhodes.

After this declaration that reiterates one of the major themes of the poem, the speaker concentrates on the sonnet's real message, which is contained in lines 10–14. These last five lines are the most quoted from "The New Colossus." They are the lines that most people remember, as well as the lines that most effectively mark the statue as the compassionate mother of all immigrants to this country. Beginning with line 10, the Statue of Liberty continues to exclaim her intention. The Statue wants to usher the people who are suffering in their lands to America, where they will be welcomed by her open arms. It is here that the statue will guard them and give them a safe place to rest. She will offer them ways to make a living and to free them from want. She suggests that those people who have gathered in frightened groups elsewhere in the world should come to the American shores, where they will find the freedoms that have been denied them. In their homelands, these people have been defined as dispensable as garbage. But this is not how the Statue of Liberty sees them. They are not enemies of this land. They are not less than any other human beings. They are merely people who are tired of war, poverty, and disease.

In line 14, the poem returns its attention to the lamp that the Statue of Liberty holds in her hand. With that torch, the Statue of Liberty not only lights the passage across the ocean and through New York Harbor, but also illuminates a special door. The speaker of this poem suggests that that door opens onto a promised land, full of hope and dreams and the means to make them come true.

Themes

Power

Different forms of power are either mentioned or alluded to in "The New Colossus." First there is power as exemplified by the ancient statue, the Colossus of Rhodes. Lazarus uses the Colossus to set up a contrast between the power exerted by warriors and conquerors and the power of mothers and nurturers. The Colossus of Rhodes represents the power of a victorious Greek god. This god, in statue form, celebrates the victory of the people of Rhodes over an army that attacked their city. The Rhodians held back the invaders and erected their colossal statue as a warning to future invaders.

There is another type of power, according to this poem, that is equally successful. This is the power of welcoming those who need help. This power is more maternal—a mother loving her children. The mother figure, as represented by the Statue of Liberty, guides her children to safety. She embraces them and welcomes them home. She does not force them. Her power is subtle, emotional, and loving.

Suffering

The suffering of those who have been exiled from their home countries, the only places they have known, is another theme of the poem. These people have been forced to leave their homeland, their friends, and, in some cases, their families. The reasons for their exiles vary. Natural disasters such as famine have driven some people to leave their countries. Others are forced to leave because they are being persecuted for their religious beliefs or their ethnicity. When they arrive in a new country, the suffering sometimes continues because many immigrants have no means of support. They are hungry, tired, and poor.

Through her poem, Lazarus suggests that the United States should help to ease the suffering of those who have been forced to leave their homelands. The poem encourages American citizens to use the Statue of Liberty as a symbol of empathy for all the suffering people who come to these shores. The immigrants should not have to suffer, this poem suggests. They have arrived in a country that has the means to ease their suffering.

Freedom

Freedom is another theme suggested in the poem. The poem implies that the Statue of Liberty is a symbol of the freedom represented by the United States and stands in contrast to the repression and war of the countries from which the immigrants have come. The old lands that once were home for these exiles are symbolized as creatures with arms made of weapons. In contrast, the new lands, such as the United States, should open their arms and beckon the immigrants to take deep breaths as they arrive and realize that they are now free.

The freedom that the poem suggests is not just religious or political freedom but also freedom from hunger and debt. Whether Lazarus believed that the United States truly represented freedom or whether she wrote the poem to encourage Americans to strive to become a model of freedom is not clear. However, she definitely describes the Statue of Liberty as a figure that, if she were able to speak, would tell immigrants that their dreams of freedom can be realized here.

Hope

The theme of hope is presented in many ways, beginning with the torch that the statue holds in her hand. The torch could represent a guiding light for those who are being tossed in the dark storms of war and poverty on the other side of the ocean. In this sense, the torch could stand for the hope of peace and safety. If readers take the torch to be a source of energy, the light could stand for a rebirth of spirit, giving hope to those who were so beaten down they were close to death. But here in America, they can begin to hope for new life.

Lazarus adds another element of hope to the end of the poem, when she mentions the symbol of the portal of gleaming gold. Not only is this an opening into a new world, it is a symbol of treasure or wealth, whether this richness is spiritual, physical, or psychological. This treasure lies behind the door. It is like the pot of gold at the end of the rainbow, something made of wishes. It is here in this country, the poem implies, that hope reigns supreme.

Topics for Further Study

- Research the history of American immigration during the last half of the nineteenth century. Who were the immigrants at that time? Where did they come from? Why were they coming to the United States? How were they treated when they arrived here? Then compare these earlier immigrant issues with those of today. Where do the largest numbers of immigrants come from today? Why do immigrants come to the United States today? How are they treated? Create a display of charts and images of your findings to use in an oral presentation to your class.

- Read about the customs and practices of Sephardic Jews. Where did they live? When and why were they banished? What became of them? How do they differ from other Jews, such as the Ashkenazic from Germany and eastern Europe and the Mizrahim from the Middle East? Gather all your information on a Web page. Include images, historical backgrounds, and cultural information. Provide maps that show where each group comes from and to which countries many of them emigrated during the twentieth century. Also collect images of special clothing, hair styles, or other elements that might distinguish one group from another. Then direct your classmates to your Web page.

- To more fully understand and appreciate Lazarus's poem, read about the experiences of immigrants. Recommended books for young adults include Janet Bode's *The Colors of Freedom: Immigrant Stories* (2000), Adele Geras's *Voyage* (2007), or Amada Irma Perez's *My Diary from Here to*

There (2002). Present your findings to your class, telling them some of the stories about what life is like for immigrants coming to America and adjusting to a new country and culture. Include personal stories if you or someone you know is an immigrant or a direct descendant of one.

- Imagine that the president of the United States has asked you to write a poem to welcome immigrants to the United States. What would be your message? Create a poem in any form you prefer (sonnet, free verse, or even a series of haiku) stating what you think the United States offers people who want to start their lives over in this country. Think about what immigrants should expect when they come here. What do you think their challenges would be today?What does America have to offer them? Read your poem to your class, or record it with background music using a computerized video or audio program, explaining that your poem will be placed next to Lazarus's poem inside the pedestal of the Statue of Liberty. Ask your classmates to compare the two poems.

- Videotape interviews with students at your school who either are immigrants or have immigrant parents. Ask them to share some of the best experiences they have had so far in their new country. Why did their parents want to come here? Have their views of the United States changed since they arrived? How? Produce a short video, upload it to YouTube, and share the results with your class.
- Create a clay figure of a modernized Statue of Liberty. Decide if this statue should be male or female and be prepared to explain why. Study the symbols that the original Statue of Liberty is holding and what they stand for. Then create symbols for your statue and tell your class why you chose them and what they represent. Keep in mind that the statue you create is supposed to greet immigrants to this country. What message do you think would make immigrants feel most welcome?

Style

Italian Sonnet

A sonnet is a special poetic form. On a basic level, the form of a sonnet consists of fourteen lines that follow a specific rhyming scheme, depending on what type of sonnet it is. The first type of sonnet was perfected by Francesco Petrarch (1304–1374), an Italian poet who used the form to write love poetry. This type of poetic form was called the Italian or Petrarchan sonnet and was adapted in the sixteenth century by the English poet Thomas Wyatt and later by William Shakespeare. Shakespeare varied the form slightly, using a different rhyme scheme that became known as the Shakespearean, or English, sonnet.

The fourteen lines of an Italian sonnet are divided into an octave, or eight lines, and a sestet, or six lines. The octave follows the rhyming pattern of *a-b-b-a, a-b-b-a* with *a* representing the first rhyme and *b* standing for the next rhyme. This means that in an Italian sonnet, the first, fourth, fifth, and eighth lines end in matching rhymes as do the second, third, sixth, and seventh lines. In the sestet, however, the rhyming pattern differs from that in the octave. The sestet rhyming pattern can follow one of several styles, most commonly either *c-d-e, c-d-e* or *c-d-c, d-c-d.*

In Lazarus's poem, lines 1, 4, 5, and 8 end in a

rhyme with a word ending with the sound "ame." Lines 2, 3, 6, and 7 end with the words ending in the sound "and." This is the conventional form of an Italian sonnet.

In the sestet, lines 9, 11, and 13 end with words rhyming with the sound of a long *e*, and lines 10, 12, and 14 end with the sound of "or." The rhyming pattern in the sestet differs from that of the octave, providing a break not only in the form but in the thought.

Traditionally, in the first section (the octave) a question is posed. In the second section (the sestet), that question is answered. The poet might also merely make a point in the octave and then emphasize that point in the sestet.

Allusion

An allusion is a literary device that makes a reference to either a historical or a literary event, person, or object that conjures up images in the reader's imagination. The use of allusion can add deeper meaning to a poem without the use of many words.

An example of an allusion in the modern world might be the World Trade Center, often referred to as the twin towers. When a writer mentions the World Trade Center, readers are reminded of the 2001 terrorist attack and all the horrors attached to this image. This image creates an emotional state of fear, anger, or sadness. Another allusion might be astronaut Neil Armstrong's landing on the moon, which represented excitement and achievement, as well as a hint of what space exploration might be like in the future.

Poets might allude to another poet's work, borrowing a few lines from a famous poem. If a poet includes the words "the road less traveled," readers familiar with the works of the American poet Robert Frost would know that the allusion was to Frost's famous "The Road Not Taken." They would also be aware of the rest of the poem and the meaning implied by these words, which accentuate the power of adventure and individuality. Some poets also make religious allusions, taking images from the Bible (such as referring to Moses as someone who leads people to the promised land).

In "The New Colossus," the colossus is an allusion to the Colossus of Rhodes, a huge male statue that once graced the harbor of the island of Rhodes in the Aegean Sea but was later destroyed by an earthquake. By making this allusion, the poet creates an image of what was one of the Seven Wonders of the ancient world—a massive structure that celebrated the successful defense of the city. Lazarus uses the allusion to bring the image of greatness into her poem in reference to the Statue of Liberty but also to bring out the contrast between the Colossus of Rhodes as a reference to war compared to the Statue of Liberty, which Lazarus saw as a symbol of peace.

Historical Context

History of the Statue of Liberty

Inspired by stories of the Colossus of Rhodes, one of the Seven Wonders of the ancient world, French sculptor Fre´ de´ ric-Auguste Bartholdi designed a statue to be given to the American people to commemorate the centennial of the Declaration of Independence. The French had helped the colonists fight the British in the American Revolution. The statue was intended to honor the friendship between France and the United States, as well as commend Americans for successfully creating a democratic government, something the French attempted to emulate in the years following the French Revolution. Alexandre-Gustave Eiffel, who designed the Eiffel Tower in Paris, constructed the framework and assisted Bartholdi in the difficult task of engineering such a huge statue.

Construction of the statue was a challenge, as was funding and transporting this great monument. The people of France were responsible for paying for the statue, while the people in the United States were asked to cover the cost of building a pedestal. Through generous donations, the money was collected and construction began. The statue was completed in 1884, and the pedestal in 1886. In order to ship the statue from France to New York

Harbor, the statue had to be reduced to 350 separate pieces. It took four months to reassemble the statue onto the pedestal in the courtyard of Fort Wood on Bedloe's Island (now Liberty Island). The statue was inaugurated on October 28, 1886, (ten years after the U.S. centennial) by President Grover Cleveland, who accepted the statue on behalf of the people of the United States.

From the ground to the tip of the torch in the statue's raised right hand measures 305 feet. There are twenty-five windows from which visitors can look out from the crown of the statue. The seven rays of the statue's crown stand for the seven seas. On the tablet that the statue holds in her left hand is inscribed the date July 4, 1776, the day on which the Second Continental Congress adopted the Declaration of Independence. The date is written in Roman numerals.

The Colossus of Rhodes

Where the Aegean Sea meets the Mediterranean at the southwestern tip of present-day Turkey is the island of Rhodes. This area was an influential economic center in the fourth and fifth centuries BCE. Many people fought for control of this port island, including leaders from Persia and Greece. When Alexander the Great, conqueror of Greece, died in 323 BCE, three Greek generals, Ptolemy, Seleucus, and Antigous, fought for control of Rhodes. When Rhodes supported Ptolemy, Antigous sent forces commanded by his son

Demetrius to conquer the city and take the Rhodian ships and port. After besieging Rhodes for a year, Demetrius was forced to give up and retreat. To celebrate, the people of Rhodes erected a huge statue to grace the harbor.

Demetrius's forces left behind many metal weapons and machinery. The people of Rhodes melted these weapons down and used the bronze to create the outer form of what would become the Colossus of Rhodes. As a frame, the Rhodians confiscated the huge tower that had used by Demetrius's army in their attempt to climb the protective walls that the Rhodians had built as part of the city's defense.

The Colossus of Rhodes was a representation of the god Helios, who was the city's patron. The statue took almost a dozen years to complete and stood from 100 to 120 feet tall exclusive of the height of the pedestal. Since the statue was destroyed by a powerful earthquake in 225 BCE, no one knows definitely what the statue looked like or where it stood at the harbor. Some have suggested that the statue was erected so that it straddled the harbors's entrance. Others have argued that this pose would have been all but impossible to construct. They suggest that, like the Statue of Liberty, the Colossus stood on one side of the harbor. Most agree that the Colossus was a great feat of construction, earning it the prestige of being called one of the seven wonders of the ancient world.

Compare & Contrast

- **1880s:** A new wave of immigrants from eastern Europe and Russia land on the East Coast of the United States in large numbers to escape escalating threats of religious and ethnic persecution and for the economic opportunities offered by the American Industrial Revolution.
- **Today:** Large populations of Hispanics from Central and South America and the Caribbean immigrate to the United States in search of jobs.
- **1880s:** France gives the Statue of Liberty to the United States as a way of expressing a friendship between the two countries that extends back to the time of the American Revolution. The statue is erected on Bedloe's Island, which is later renamed Liberty Island, in New York Harbor.
- **Today:** The Statue of Liberty is closed after the terrorist attacks on the World Trade Center on September 11, 2001. The pedestal and outdoor observation decks reopened in 2004. On July 4, 2009, the crown on the head of the statue is finally reopened to visitors.
- **1880s:** Lazarus is considered the most recognized Jewish female poet

of her time.

- **Today:** After being awarded prestigious prizes that include the MacArthur Fellowship (1994), the Wallace Stevens Award (1996), and the Lifetime Achievement Award from the Lannan Foundation (1999), Adrienne Rich, one of the most noted Jewish female poets of today, is honored with the Griffin Poetry Prize (2010) in recognition of her lifetime work.

U.S. Immigration, 1880–1920

In the early 1800s, most immigrants to the United States came from northern and western Europe. Hoping to escape hunger from massive crop failures and revolution, large populations, especially from Ireland and Germany, fled to North America. Between 1830 and 1860, immigrants to the United States numbered almost 5 million. After 1860, because of the U.S. Civil War, the number of immigrants dropped significantly except for Chinese laborers who arrived on the West Coast to help build the transcontinental railroad.

In the 1880s, the immigrant population swelled again. Between 1880 and 1920, almost 24 million new immigrants arrived in the United States. Where as prior to the Civil War most immigrants came from western and northern Europe and China, people seeking refuge in America now. came from southern and eastern Europe, and Russia. Lack of jobs in eastern Europe as well as the persecution of Jews were two major reasons for the mass immigration. Most immigrants settled in the major cities in the northeast and in Chicago, where they found jobs in factories that provided work but very low wages. Many of these new immigrants lived in poverty, in crowded housing called tenements that had little provision for sanitation. As a result, diseases spread throughout the communities. Poor health and poor pay led some to crime in order to survive. The general attitude of the American public toward these large numbers of immigrants was not positive. Many people blamed them for taking jobs away and for wreaking havoc on the city environment.

Listening to the public outcries against immigrants, the U.S. Congress passed new laws in 1882 that controlled the numbers and the types of immigrants allowed into the country. Criminals and those with certain diseases were not allowed to enter. In addition, taxes were imposed, forcing immigrants to hand over money, which many of them did not have. Those who could not pay were forced to return to the country they had come from. Finally, in 1924, Congress passed another Immigration Act that further limited the number of immigrants entering the United States by instituting a quota system (meaning that only a limited number from each country were allowed in).

Critical Overview

Esther Schor, in her biography *Emma Lazarus* writes that "The New Colossus," when chosen for the pedestal, "transformed" the Statue of Liberty from a symbol of freedom to "a new sort of colossus altogether." The poem relieved the statue "of a heavy inheritance of tyranny," which was what the Colossus of Rhodes stood for. After being placed in the pedestal, Lazarus's poem was "mentioned widely in the press," Schor says. She also quotes James Russell Lowell, an American poet, who likens Lazarus's poem to a "'noble' pedestal for the statue." Lowell writes that Lazarus used "just the right word to be said, an achievement more arduous than that of the sculptor" of the statue.

In his review of the poem, David Lehman, writing for *Smithsonian* states: "There is no more memorable statement of… the American dream than the promise of safe haven," which Lazarus's poem voices. Lehman adds that the poem is not a "boast but [rather] a vow." The focus of the poem is not on a "glorification of the self but on the rescue of others." Lehman also praises Lazarus herself, writing that she was a "much more substantial poet than she has been given credit for."

In her review for *Shofar*, Wendy Zierler says that Lazarus's poem is a powerful voice, especially for female poets who are inspired not by "classical, patriarchal traditions," but by feelings for the "oppressed or marginalized people of the world."

Reviews written in Lazarus's day tend to praise her work, though they do so in a somewhat patronizing manner. A reviewer for the *Nation* says that Lazarus's poems "indicate more than common ability." Another critic, writing for *Galaxy* reports that Lazarus's poetry has qualities that "distinguish it broadly from the ordinary work of women," as well as from "the best work of most young writers."

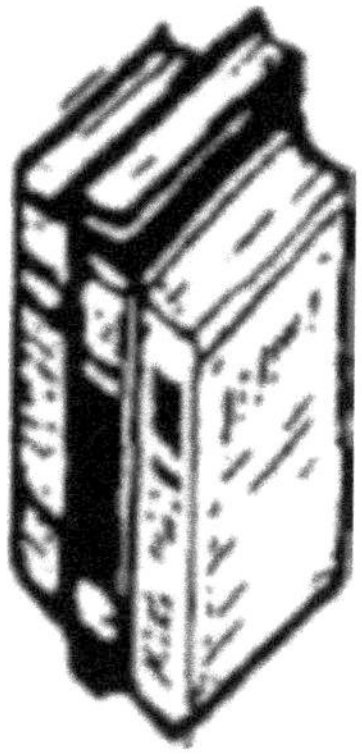

What Do I Read Next?

- *Emma Lazarus: Selected Poems* (2005) includes many of Lazarus's poems that did not gain the widespread fame of "The New Colossus." Her poems in this collection focus on the casualties of the U.S. Civil War and on immigration to America, with a special emphasis on the lives of Jewish people. Some of the outstanding poems included in this collection are “Heroes” and “The Day of Dead Soldiers,” both of which deal with war. Other poems are “On the Jewish New Year” and “In Exile,” which focus on Jewish issues.

- Hannia S. Moore has written a fictional account of Lazarus's life in her novel *Liberty's Poet: Emma Lazarus* (2005). Moore creates a fictionalized version of Lazarus as a young girl born to a wealthy Jewish family in the United States in the 1800s. The story features a young poet who is befriended by none other than Ralph Waldo Emerson, the noted poet.
- Young-adult readers might enjoy *Emma Lazarus Rediscovered* (1999) by the poet Eve Merriam. This book was originally published in 1956 but was republished as a tribute to Lazarus during the celebration of the 150th anniversary of her birth. The book includes an introduction by Morris Schappes, who has done extensive studies of Lazarus's life and work.
- The American poet Ralph Waldo

Emerson served as a mentor to Lazarus for many years, influencing the form and content of her writing. In *The Essential Writings of Ralph Waldo Emerson* (2000) readers gain an understanding of his style of writing as well as the underlying concepts and themes of his work.

- For a different view of immigration, read Jack Marshall's *From Baghdad to Brooklyn: Growing Up in a Jewish-Arabic Family in Mid-century America* (2005). This coming-of-age memoir received a starred review from *Publishers Weekly*. In this book, Ralph Waldo Emerson's poetry becomes a heavy influence on the young boy's life.
- Born around the time of Lazarus's death, Isaac Rosenberg, whose parents were Jewish immigrants to the United Kingdom, based much of his poetry on his experiences in World War I. He is often referred to as the best war poet of his generation. Though Lazarus wrote about war from a spectator's standpoint, Rosenberg had firsthand experiences. For a long time, the only published copies of Rosenberg's poetry were in the form of pamphlets that the poet self-

published. *Selected Poems and Letters*, published in 2004, is a good source for his work.

- For young or second-language readers, Linda Glaser has written the book *Emma's Poem: The Voice of the Statue of Liberty* (2010). The story of Lazarus and her famous poem is told through words and illustrations.

Sources

Ambrose, Stephen E., *Nothing Like It in the World: The Men Who Built the Transcontinental Railroad, 1863–1869*, Simon & Schuster, 2000.

Byers, Ann, *The History of U.S. Immigration: Coming to America*, Enslow Publishers, 2006.

Curlee, Lynn, *The Seven Wonders of the Ancient World*, Atheneum, 2002, pp. 24–26.

Dubnow, Simon, *History of the Jews in Russia and Poland, Vol. 3 of 3: From the Earliest Times Until the Present Day*, Forgotten Books, 2010, pp. 66–101.

Frost, Robert, *The Road Not Taken: A Selection of Robert Frost's Poems*, Holt Paperbacks, 2nd rev. ed., 2002, p. 270.

"Immigration, The Journey to America, The Chinese," in *Oracle ThinkQuest Education Foundation*, http://library.thinkquest.org/20619/Chinese.html (accessed May 24, 2010).

Lazarus, Emma, "The New Colossus," in *Emma Lazarus, Selected Poems*, edited by John Hollander, Library of America, 2005, p. 58.

Lehman, David, "Colossal Ode," in *Smithsonian*, Vol. 35, No. 1, April 2004, pp. 120–22.

Review of *Admetus, and Other Poems*, in *Galaxy*, Vol. 13, No. 1, January 1872, pp. 136–37.

Review of *Admetus, in Nation*, Vol. 14, No. 345, February 8, 1872, p. 92.

Schor, Esther, *Emma Lazarus*, Schocken Books, 2006, pp. 188, 191.

"Statue of Liberty," in *National Park Service*, http://www.nps.gov/stli/index.htm (accessed on May 25, 2010).

Zierler, Wendy, "The Making and Re-Making of Jewish-American Literary History," in *Shofar*, Vol. 27, No. 2, Winter 2009, p. 69.

Further Reading

Ash, Russell, *Great Wonders of the World*, DK Children, 2000.

Ash focuses his attention in this young-adult book on many spectacular accomplishments in history. The Colossus of Rhodes is included, along with more generalized categories, such as the great accomplishments in engineering, inventions, and special phenomena in the natural world.

Bray, Ilona, J.D., *U.S. Immigration Made Easy*, 14th ed., updated by Jeptha Evans and Ruby Lieberman, NOLO, 2009.

Using topics such as how to begin your journey toward immigration, dealing with the paperwork involved, finding a lawyer, and obtaining a green card, the authors of this book (all lawyers) provide information about how to immigrate to the United States.

Coan, Peter Morton, *Ellis Island Interviews: In Their Own Words*, Facts on File, 1997.

Coan explores the history of Ellis Island, where immigrants, especially between 1892 and 1924, first landed in the States. Interviews with more than 130 different people from Europe and the Middle East, some of them famous, most of them not, heighten the emotional content of the reading.

Gallo, Donald, *First Crossing: Stories about Teen Immigrants*, Candlewick, 2007.

In this young-adult collection, Gallo presents stories about the experiences of contemporary teenagers who have immigrated to the United States. The stories focus on a wide variety of teens, from those being smuggled across the border from Mexico to the culture clash experienced by a teen attempting to adjust after moving to the United States from Korea.

Hammerschmidt, Peter A., *History of American Immigration*, Mason Crest, 2009.

In this young-adult book, Hammerschmidt examines the history of immigration in the United States, demonstrating how diverse the people of this country are. Describing various cultures and customs, he explores the influence of immigrants on American life.

Khan, Yasmin Sabina, *Enlightening the World: The Creation of the Statue of Liberty*, Cornell University

Press, 2010.

Khan provides an history of the Statue of Liberty, recounting the reasons behind France's creation of this gift to the United States. She describes the work of the French sculptor Auguste Bartholdi and the fundraising work of American publisher Joseph Pulitzer to pay for the pedestal, and gives details about Emma Lazarus's life.

Polacheck, Hilda Satt, *I Came a Stranger: The Story of a Hull-House Girl*, edited by Dena J. Polacheck Epstein, University of Illinois Press, 1989.

In this memoir, Polacheck recounts her immigration to Chicago from Poland. Polacheck was a young Jewish woman when she arrived. Later in life, she wrote her story but could not find a publisher. She died without knowing that her work was finally put into book form through the efforts of her granddaughter.

Suggested Search Terms

Emma Lazarus

The New Colossus

Statue of Liberty

history of U.S. immigration

Liberty Island

Lazarus and Statue of Liberty

Lazarus and Jewish literature

female Jewish poets

Ralph Waldo Emerson and Emma Lazarus

Immigration and Naturalization Service

Ellis Island

Lightning Source UK Ltd.
Milton Keynes UK
UKHW020803121222
413794UK00015B/1023

9 781375 392723